HOCKEY *TIPS* FROM THE *PROS*

ZIGGY PALFFY

HOCKEY THE NHL® WAY

**Sean Rossiter
& Paul Carson**

Hockey
Tips from the
pros

GREYSTONE BOOKS

Douglas & McIntyre Publishing Group

Vancouver/Toronto/New York

Greystone Books
A division of Douglas & McIntyre Ltd.
2323 Quebec Street, Suite 201
Vancouver, British Columbia
Canada V5T 4S7
www.greystonebooks.com

National Library of Canada Cataloguing in Publication Data
Rossiter, Sean, 1946 –
    Hockey tips from the pros
    (Hockey the NHL way)

    ISBN 1-55054-864-6

    1. Hockey—Juvenile literature. I. Carson, Paul, 1955–
II. Title. III. Series
GV847.25.R683 2001   j796.962   C2001-910311-5

Editing by Lucy Kenward
Cover and text design by Peter Cocking
Front cover photograph by Bruce Bennett/
Bruce Bennett Studios
Printed and bound in Canada by Friesens
Printed on acid-free paper ∞

Every reasonable care has been taken to trace the ownership of copyrighted visual material. Information that will enable the publishers to rectify any reference or credit is welcome.

The publisher gratefully acknowledges the assistance of the Canada Council and of the British Columbia Ministry of Tourism, Small Business and Culture. The publisher also acknowledges the financial support of the Government of Canada through the Book Publishing Industry Development Program (BPIDP) for its publishing activities.

CREDITS
Photography
Photos by Bruce Bennett Studios:
pp. i, 13, 14, 52: Jim Leary · pp. ii, 10, 16, 21, 28, 45, 54: Bruce Bennett · p. 4: Peter MacCallum · pp. 6, 50: John Giamundo · pp. 8, 19, 23, 30, 32, 38, 46: Jim McIsaac · p. 9: Henry DiRocco · pp. 20, 58: Claus Andersen · p. 24: Andy Marlin · pp. 26, 27, 57: Mark Buckner · pp. 33, 42: Doug MacMillan · p. 34: Brian Winkler · p. 53: Art Foxall

Photos © NHL Images:
p. 37: Tim DeFrisco · p. 41: Craig Melvin · p. 44: Dave Sandford · p. 49: Kent Smith

Photo on p. 2 by Jamie Sabau/Columbus Blue Jackets

NHL Player Quotes
Peter Bondra: Rachel Alexander, "Quietly, Bondra Carries a Big Stick; Without Fanfare, Cap Leads NHL in Goals, Team into the Playoffs," *Washington Post,* 21 April 1998.

Jaromir Jagr: Dejan Kovacevic, "Jagr's Game Still Not Four-Star," *Pittsburgh Post-Gazette,* 22 November 2000.

Scott Young: Larry Wigge, "The Sporting News," *St. Louis Post-Dispatch,* 8 November 2000.

Marc Crawford: Steve Snelgrove, "Aucoin Finding Scoring Touch," *Vancouver Sun,* 4 January 2001. ("Confidence . . . earn it." only)

Mario Lemieux: Dave Molinari, "Penguins Notebook: Lemieux Adjusting to New Faces, Places," *Pittsburgh Post-Gazette,* 9 January 2001.

Bob Boughner: Dejan Kovacevic, "Penguins Report," *Pittsburgh Post-Gazette,* 9 November 2000.

Ziggy Palffy: Jim Hodges, "Palffy Principle: Game's the Thing," *Los Angeles Times,* 5 December 2000.

Rick Tocchet: Larry Wigge, "As Senators Win, Yashin Skates Alone," *The Sporting News,* 24 October 2000.

Darius Kasparaitis: Dave Molinari, "Penguins Can Expect Heavy Dose of Snow," *Pittsburgh Post-Gazette,* 5 December 2000.

Dennis Bonvie: Dave Molinari, "3-Line Rotation Puts Kraft in Dock," *Pittsburgh Post-Gazette,* 13 October 2000.

contents

foreword

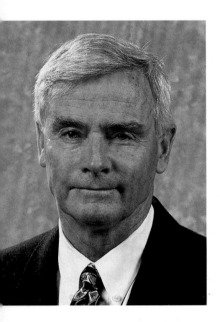

As a National Hockey League coach, I see every day how certain players can handle the puck as if on a string, or make laser passes through forests of legs or score seeing-eye goals that nobody else could even imagine. I get a kick out of watching those players. They make the hockey fan in me shout with joy.

I have seen players who could work that magic play only a few games in the NHL. Others go on to have long, productive careers. Some are in the Hockey Hall of Fame.

What's the difference? That's a good question. If I knew for sure, I would make the Blue Jackets the newest expansion team ever to win a Stanley Cup. The more I think about it, the more I believe the difference between players with equal skills who are in the NHL, and those with the same skills who don't stay in the league, is a very simple thing.

The ones in the NHL love the game. NHL players are not the only ones who love hockey, but all of them grew up wanting to know everything there is to know about the game. They have given up a lot of the good things in life to play at this level. Game in and game out, they perform acts of great courage that are often kept secret. Some of them quietly put up with pain that would cripple most people. You've got to love a game that costs so much to play.

On the other hand, most NHL players will tell you that they are thrilled to be paid for playing a game they would play for free. They enjoy being in the dressing room, laughing with their teammates. They respect their opponents, because without special opponents you can't have a great game. And, somehow, because they pay attention all the time, they also figure out all the little things that make all the difference in hockey. Hockey offers dozens of small rewards, such as finding the perfect stick among dozens or making the tape-to-tape first pass out of your zone that only your teammates notice. Like all hockey players, NHL players get a kick out of stepping on the ice when it's perfect. They know what can be done on it.

Physical skills matter in hockey. It's a skill game. But what you can do with the puck is not everything. Only one player can have the puck at any one time. What about the other nine players on the ice? They, too, have roles. How well you play your role without the puck can set you apart. There's plenty to hockey besides stickhandling, playmaking and shooting the puck.

This book is about puckhandling skills, but it is also about those other things NHL players do that get them to the top and keep them there. It's about that sixth hockey sense, something we call hockey smarts. We sometimes call them "the little things." The things that are hard to see but make all the difference. We could call them secrets.

These are the secrets of life in the NHL— revealed in the players' own words.

Dave King (signature)

Dave King
Head Coach, Columbus Blue Jackets

SHAWN McEACHERN

introduction

This book is the result of talking with more than 125 active National Hockey League players. We asked them specific questions about how they use their speed to create scoring chances, what they do to play their best, game after game, and how they work with their teammates to win games. We asked about the mental and the physical aspects of the game. We asked for their favourite playing tips—tips as specific as how goaltenders should poke-check.

We have arranged this gold mine of NHL playing tips in a new way. The tips are not listed by skills, but by aspects of the game that go far past physical skills. We asked players who have had Hockey Hall of Fame careers to tell us what went into their success. We asked role players how they stay in the NHL. These answers are arranged—not by skills or by positions—but by types of players: from goal scorers to checking super-pests, speedsters to team players. We even consider goaltenders to be hockey players. They, too, can be speedy and agile. A few goalies even score goals.

So the book you hold in your hands is a unique set of personal snapshots of life in the NHL, in the players' own words. It's about life on and off the ice, how to learn hockey skills and how to perform them in games, how to provide leadership in the dressing room and how to fit in with the team.

But what the NHL players' answers tell us is something even more important than the information they contain. They tell us something about those players that very few of them would ever say about themselves.

The most important secret in *Hockey the NHL Way: Tips From the Pros* is no real secret at all. The ones who are consistent, who play big and who are team players, are the ones who love the game the most. For them, whatever it takes to play at the highest level is what they will do.

That's what this book is all about—how NHL players express their love of hockey, game by game, every night of the season.

goal scoring

▲ PAVEL BURE

Goals are what bring 18,000 fans to their feet in National Hockey League arenas. Garbage goals, fat rebounds, deflections off a defenseman's skate—they all count. An end-to-end rush is more of a thrill, but they don't give bonus points in hockey for looking good. Goals are the only numbers left on the scoreboard after a game. Add them up, see who wins.

It's true that hockey is more than just scoring goals. Goals are scored by single players, but most goals result from the efforts of more than one teammate. That's why assists are awarded—usually more than one.

Goals start with checking. You have to get the puck before you can score. That means doing a lot of little things right, such as covering your check in your own zone. It means skating into position to receive the first pass out of your zone when you see your team is about to get the puck. It means digging the puck out of the corners in the offensive zone.

Fewer goals were scored in the NHL during the 1990s because teams knew that, to win, they had to stop their opponents from scoring. One outcome of better defense is that the goals that are scored are more important.

With goals being such a big deal, why are there no goal-scoring coaches? In fact, very few goal scorers ever become coaches. Many hockey people say that goal scoring cannot be taught.

So we asked top scorers how they do it. No two gave the same answer. But they did offer tips that can improve your puck luck.

Bobby Holik shot hundreds of pucks daily as a youngster. Joe Sakic says shoot quickly, before the goalie is ready. John LeClair says you can't score unless you hit the net. Pavel Bure, who gets lots of breakaways, says when it's you and the goalie, go with your instinct—just react. Michael York says always play heads-up: look for rebounds, expect the unexpected. Mario Lemieux likes to study goalies. Tony Amonte says that top scorers think about scoring all the time.

The question is as old as the game itself. Are goal scorers born or made? Can you make yourself into a scorer? Nobody really knows.

What we can say is that, based on the advice of NHL snipers, every top scorer is different. So read these tips. And practise, practise, practise.

It's all in your head, TONY AMONTE says:

"I think scoring is more a state of mind than anything else. You've got to want to score. If you think about it all the time, you will score. And that's what the game's all about."

Speed = goals, by PETER BONDRA:

"I shoot the puck a lot, and I get good chances because I skate fast. When you get to the puck quickly, you have a half step on the defender and that gives you time to look at the goalie and know what his position is. You get time to know where to shoot and to take the shot you want."

TEEMU SELANNE takes a good look: ➤

"When you shoot, you want to see how far the goalie is going to come out. All goalies have different styles of play: some go down right away, some play more of a stand-up style and others use the butterfly. It helps to know, before the game, what style the goalie uses."

◄ MICHAEL YORK knows the score:

"To be an effective goal scorer, you've always got to keep your head in the game and always be ready to pounce on the loose puck. Go to the net, have your stick on the ice and keep your head up. If you aren't paying attention, you're going to miss great scoring chances."

PAVEL BURE on the one-on-one instinct:

"On a breakaway, you just react. You don't really decide whether to shoot or to deke. It happens so quickly—you just react. You don't really have time to think, because somebody's chasing you. And if you take time to think, you'll get in too close to the goalie. I guess you just see what's open and try to create something."

◄ **Speedster SAKU KOIVU's breakaway tip:**

"When I get a breakaway, I have a couple of moves in my mind. It depends on the goalie we're playing against, on the angle that I'm cutting to the net and on the speed— all those things. You have to see who the goalie is and how much time you have, and then you just react."

Goalie ROMAN TUREK on breakaways versus penalty shots:

"Playing a breakaway is different than a penalty shot. On a penalty shot, the player has a lot more time. On a break-away, I try not to make the first move—I wait for the shooter to make it and then react to his move."

How MARIUSZ CZERKAWSKI became a sniper:

"In the summertime, I had a rubber mat out in the backyard, and I painted spots on a wall that I wanted to hit. Even on a nice sunny day, I was out working on my shot, taking as many shots as I could. Sometimes during practice you don't have extra guys there to check you, but you should still try to take the shots as quickly as you can. Try to surprise the goalie."

BOBBY HOLIK says practice makes perfect:
"When I was growing up, I worked on my shot every day, shooting hundreds of pucks every day. Summer or winter, whether it was on the ice or on a plastic board, it was just shoot, shoot, shoot. Practise—there's nothing you can do to improve your shot except practise shooting."

Confidence helps CAMMI GRANATO of the U.S. National Women's team:
"I don't have the hardest shot, but I feel confident when shooting the puck. The more confidence you have, the bigger the net becomes, and that confidence can make a big difference in your scoring ability. Some people have a scoring touch that comes naturally, but others can learn to score. You can improve your puck luck by taking extra shots in practice and by becoming stronger."

One-on-one, by MIROSLAV SATAN: ➤
"When you skate in on a breakaway, look to see what the goalie is giving you. If he leaves a big hole to shoot at, take it. If he isn't giving you anything, then you have to create your own opening by making a move to get the goalie out of position."

How CASSIE CAMPBELL of the Canadian National Women's team learned to score:
"To score, you have to be ready to shoot at all times. As you gain experience, you learn to check the goalie's position in the net and to look for angles. Being able to look like you're going to pass rather than shoot can also be helpful when trying to score, and a quick release can help with this kind of deception.

"If you ask goaltenders which is the most difficult shot to stop, they would say the backhand. A slap shot may be the hardest one a player can take, but it allows the goalie time to get ready for the save."

Point man ADRIAN AUCOIN says keep your shot low:

"If you keep your shot from the point low—not necessarily on the ice but maybe a foot or two high—it definitely helps your players to deflect the puck. Nowadays, some butterfly goalies cover the ice quite well, that's why if your shot's a foot or two high, the chances are better that it will go in.

"The power of my slap shot comes mostly from my legs, but a lot of it also comes from timing, leverage and getting the right amount of ice. A lot of people try to hit the puck cleanly off the ice, but you have to hit the ice just behind the puck to get the whip of your stick."

◄ JAROMIR JAGR tells how he became a top scorer:

"I'm hard on myself, and my dad was hard on me. And that's what got me to where I'm at right now, so I don't know any other way. You know how hard you can push, and only you know how good you can be if you push yourself. I know that, and that's why I'm pushing myself."

How power forward JOHN LECLAIR scores from close in:

"When you're on the lip of the crease, by just moving your stick or moving your feet you can get the puck to a different angle and beat the goaltender. Aside from that, hit the net. Anything can happen when you hit the net."

ERIC DAZE uses power and speed:

"I like to stay in front of the net and try to get a rebound, but every player is different depending on their strength. I try to shoot as quickly as possible to surprise the goalie. And I don't even look where I'm shooting most of the time. It's just power and speed."

PAUL COFFEY's skating secrets:

"If I told you my secret about skating, it wouldn't be a secret! Seriously, though, it's hard work. A lot of it is natural ability, no doubt about that, but you have to build your leg strength and you have to keep your conditioning high. You also need to make sure that your skates, which are the most important part of your equipment, are sharp and ready to go."

Speed comes first, says BRIAN ROLSTON:

"You can work to develop your speed, but it's usually something that you're born with—you either have it or you don't. If you don't have speed, you have to work on your other skills."

How defender SCOTT NIEDERMAYER keeps the jets on: ➤

"I like to keep my speed and not lose it, and maybe circle behind the net and build up speed from there—as opposed to a forward who might use his quickness in and out of the corners."

SHAWN McEACHERN says move your feet:

"As a young player, you have to get your legs stronger. Quickness is a key that you should work on during practices as well. During games, it's important that when you get the puck, you get your legs moving and use your speed when you can."

ARTURS IRBE says be flexible:

"It's best to start stretching when you're young. There's never a limit, especially when your body is still growing. Once you're grown up, though, the room for improvement is very slight."

TREVOR LETOWSKI turns the tables on the power play:

"You're out there to do one job, and that's to kill off the penalty. It's good to have speed, but it's more important to work on cutting off the angles. It's all about working hard, and if you do, the big shorthanded goals will come."

Short and straight = control, by ADAM OATES:

"Using a shorter stick is a habit that I got into a long time ago, and I'm now very comfortable with it. One advantage for a centre using a straighter blade is that it enables you to pass on your forehand and on your backhand. That's something all centres need to be able to do."

MARTIN BRODEUR, top-scoring goalie: ➤

"I work at handling the puck a lot in practices, in the street, anywhere I can. I love to control and play the puck. It's just a matter of reading the play and having the confidence to do it."

How goalie BRENT JOHNSON watches the puck behind the net:

"If the puck is behind the net, you don't want to face the guy with the puck. You always want to be aware of where the puck is—you can look behind the net—but you never want to turn your back on the players in front of the net."

Goalie EVGENI NABOKOV, on using the poke-check:

"Before you poke-check, you've got to see if the forward is looking at you or not. If the forward is looking at the puck, that's a good moment for the poke-check. But if the forward is looking at you and you go to the poke-check, he's got you."

consistency

▲ JASON ARNOTT & JOE SAKIC

Many fine hockey players never make it to the National Hockey League. There's no shame in that. Very few do make the NHL. What is sad is that many of the players who don't make it have NHL skills. But they don't show those skills in every game. The ability to play hard, play smart and play big, game after game, is what separates players with equal skills at every level, from Atom to the pros.

Hockey players are not robots. We get hurt. We get sick. We have things on our minds. But if your coach can count on you to play your best—even when you don't feel like it—you'll get plenty of ice time wherever you play.

Being consistent means more than just wanting to bring your A game to the rink every time. You have to organize your life around the things you want to do well. Take care of yourself. Maintain a high level of fitness with aerobic exercise, such as running or swimming. (Think about weight training only after you have finished growing.) Get your rest. Eat right. Have your injuries treated properly. Learn how to deal with minor scrapes yourself.

Often the key to being ready for each game is your mental preparation. Try to give yourself a pre-game routine that you follow game-in and game-out. (Goalies often start thinking about upcoming games the day before.) The idea is to get ready for the game the same way each time.

Such a routine could begin with assembling your equipment. NHL players spend hours working on sticks each game day. Packing your equipment bag a few hours before the game gives you a chance to see that everything is shipshape—with time left for repairs if necessary. Build in some time to think about the game. Think about what you'd like to do on the ice. Visualize yourself going to the net, or deciding whether to pinch at the offensive blue line, or taking faceoffs or making certain kinds of saves. Imagine exactly how you will do these things, step by step. Before you go to the rink, do your stretching.

Leave lots of time to get to the rink early. Never rush dressing for the game.

Those are a few things you can do to put your best foot forward when you step out on that fresh, mirror-like ice. It's your stage.

World and Stanley Cup champion IGOR LARIONOV:

"Hockey is like life: there's no room to be satisfied. There are high demands, and you have to set a certain level for yourself, and you have to be consistent. You have to prepare yourself mentally to play every night, and you have to give the best performance you can."

ROB NIEDERMAYER on the pre-game meal:

"It's important to get the right food in you before a game. It plays a big part in how much energy you have. Before a 7:30 game, I eat between 12:30 and 1:00. Usually, I have some chicken and some pasta. I have a little snack—a bagel or something like that—around 4:30 or 5:00.

"After the game, refuel your body. About a half hour after you exercise, replenish your carbohydrates with a bagel, pasta or some fruit. I usually have a sports drink after as well."

PIERRE TURGEON has a plan: ➤

"To be consistent, I try not to focus on what is going to happen in the future but, rather, on the particular moment and the particular play."

◄ CHRIS PRONGER learns from the best:

"What I've learned from playing with great veterans is consistency. They come to the rink every day, prepared for the practice and games. You learn just being around the guys in the locker room."

What makes ADAM GRAVES play hard night after night:
"We've got the greatest jobs in the world as NHL players, and being able to do what you love is always fun. I never take for granted the love of the game and how lucky I am to be able to play in the league."

VINCENT DAMPHOUSSE takes off the gloves:
"My consistency for scoring points has come from not missing too many games. I've never had any really great seasons, but I've been lucky to stay away from injuries. One thing that might help me is that I like new equipment. I like to have new gloves almost every three months."

◄ **Competing game after game, by MARK RECCHI:**
"There are nights when you don't feel that great, but you have to be able to suck it up and play for your teammates and for your team. You have to sacrifice yourself every night. If you can play that way, you can become a pretty consistent player."

How goalie JOSE THEODORE handles bad goals:
"It all depends when you let the bad goal in. If it's early in the first period, you say 'Forget about it.' If that's the only goal you let in, there's a good chance you're going to win the game. If it's at the end of the game, and you lose the game, then you try to bounce back the next game."

KIM ST-PIERRE, Canadian National Women's team goalie:
"If you can learn the basic techniques then you'll be successful, and success means fun. By working on the basic stance, always keeping your stick on the ice and being square to the puck, any goalie—boy or girl—will be successful."

hockey
smarts

▲ PAUL KARIYA & ERIC DESJARDINS

You've seen it. Some players have all the luck. The puck follows them around the ice. They are always where the action is. They know the game in ways that other players do not. They have what are called hockey smarts, or puck luck.

How can you learn that stuff? Some young players hang out at rinks and in dressing rooms, watching every game they can find and playing with older players when they can. You don't learn—at least, not like in school—as much as you breathe the air and keep your eyes open. Ask questions. Listen.

Some National Hockey League players, such as Anson Carter and Ray Whitney, believe these secrets cannot be learned. You either know them or you don't. There is no set of lessons that coaches use to teach hockey smarts. Whitney calls it anticipation. That means knowing what will happen next on the ice.

But, for other players like Simon Gagne, a lot about the game can be learned. Cammi Granato, of the U.S. National Women's Team, learned a lot from her brother, NHLer Tony Granato. Just looking around an NHL dressing room tells you a lot about hockey: how equipment is stored, where the goalies dress, what the coach writes on the blackboard. You get a sense of the little things that go into making our game great.

Walter Gretzky taught his son Wayne at a very young age to read the play so that he could tell where the puck was about to go. That way young Wayne could skate to where the puck was going to be, rather than follow it around. He could be there, waiting, when the puck arrived. Soon the lessons became instinct.

What these players have in common is a love for the game that makes them want to know everything about hockey. Jacques Plante, the Hockey Hall of Famer and father of the goalie's mask, advised goalies to learn from every goaltender they play against, good or bad. Plante's idea was that you should be learning all the time, all your life, without being taught. So be a student of the game. Talk hockey with your coach.

Which brings us to Hockey Secret #1. Hockey is a game. Games should be fun. If you are not having fun playing hockey, you won't take in all those hockey smarts that can't be taught.

Talent versus learning, by SIMON GAGNE:

"For me, everything is learned, including hockey sense. When I was young, I watched Joe Sakic and I tried to be like him. And I learned a lot from my coaches when I was in junior. You have to learn to get in position for a rebound."

Learning the game, by PHIL HOUSLEY:

"At a young age, it's very important to get as much ice time as you can, whether it's with your organized team or skating outside with your friends. You pick up a lot of your skills and the fundamentals of the game while practising."

ANSON CARTER on anticipation: ➤

"I think hockey sense is something that comes naturally. You either know the game or you don't. If you aren't blessed with a lot of hockey sense, you can certainly overcome any deficiencies with hard work and dedication."

◄ **RAY WHITNEY on the waiting game:**

"Anticipation—knowing where the puck is going, rather than where it's been—is an important part of the game. You have to learn the game and understand the game. I've never been taught anything on anticipation. You either understand the game and what the players' options are, or you don't."

JYRKI LUMME makes time to practise:

"When I was young, I always had my own time before and after practice to spend on my stickhandling. At times, I was all by myself late at night, trying different moves. I would act like one of the players that I idolized growing up. You need to make your own time if you want to be one of the best."

◄ **CAMMI GRANATO on having a brother in the NHL:**

"My brother Tony has given me loads of advice over the years, and I always took it very seriously: Always work your hardest. Listen, and learn from those around you. Be a team player—respect your teammates and your coach. Be confident yet humble. Never get complacent, always try to get better. Most importantly, have fun."

STEVE KARIYA on the big brother thing:

"I've always tried to be my own player on the ice and my own person off the ice. My brother has been a tremendous asset to me—he has taught me how hard you need to work to become an NHL player. Work hard on your skills, have fun and don't worry about any comparisons to older brothers or other players."

PAUL KARIYA's advice for life:

"Focus on the task at hand. It doesn't matter what the task is, whether it's designing a play, riding the exercise bike or lifting weights."

JEFF FRIESEN on doing the little things right:

"Keys to the NHL game are to work along the boards—getting pucks out and getting them in—at both blue lines."

The advice coach PAT QUINN gives young defensemen:

"The first piece of advice I give defensemen is to learn proper stick position. Too often they play with two hands on the stick when only one should be used to get proper position against an attacker. The second piece of advice is to be prepared to move the puck before you get to it, because the first pass is the most important part of getting the puck out of your own zone."

What RICK GREEN, assistant coach, teaches his defenders:

"With my defensemen, I stress four things: proper technique for body checking, keeping their sticks on the ice, playing the angles and protecting the front of the net—you see a tendency for some of them to do a lot of wandering around and not be aware of their positioning. Those are the things I would teach youngsters—we're still doing it at the NHL level."

ROB BLAKE on the first rule of defense: ➤

"In your own end, it's important to keep your body between the player and the net. If the puck gets behind you, don't let the player get behind you."

KEN DANEYKO on when to turn with the puck carrier:

"When I'm defending against the rush, I turn on the puck carrier when I feel he has a step on me. It's a matter of timing and knowing who's fast and who's not."

ERIC WEINRICH says be ahead of the play:

"One of my coaches told me that as a defenseman you never want to be chasing the play back into your end, but always skating backward and in front of the play. If you're going to play defense, play defense first."

ROB ZAMUNER on being a good defensive forward:

"You can leave your check when you see there is a breakdown in coverage and someone else has a better scoring opportunity than the man you're checking. You can also leave your check when your defenseman has full control of the puck, and your team begins the transition from defense to offense. That way you're creating an outlet pass for your teammate."

◄ MARIO LEMIEUX is still learning:

"Obviously, when you know what the other team's going to do, and especially certain players, it's to your advantage. When I'm on the bench, I watch their defensemen: how they skate and how they react to certain situations. I watch the defensemen more than forwards and, of course, the goalies. I like to study goalies."

A defensive tip from KELLY BUCHBERGER:

"Most significantly you always have to be on the defensive side of your check. You can't give them much room because there are very skilled players in this league who can dangle the puck, so you have to get in front of them as much as possible."

How SCOTT YOUNG became a scorer:

"Maybe I'm getting smarter in my old age. In the past I used to skate like 100 mph from one spot to another—and not accomplish as much as I'd like. Now I think I'm playing smarter. I'm looking for the openings and sitting there waiting for the puck, not running around like a crazy man."

DAVE NONIS, hockey executive:

"Before we draft a player, we go to his old teams and look at the roles he's played. Is he a leader? Does he play hard both on the road and at home, night in and night out? Is he well respected by his coaches and teammates? If you do that background work, you can discern the guys who are willing to do whatever it takes to win. Those are the guys who generally make up winning teams."

DOUG WEIGHT on pre-game mental preparation:

"Visualization helps improve your confidence, and it makes tasks easier because you are reacting in situations rather than thinking. I visualize certain aspects of my game, including faceoffs, body control and puck movement. In the case of faceoffs, I visualize winning draws against centres I might face that night. For body control, I focus mainly on foot movement as I'm moving in on a defenseman. I also key in on puck movement in power-play situations."

Give yourself a break, by JOE NIEUWENDYK: ➤
"When I was young, I played lacrosse in the summertime. Hockey should be played for fun— but when it isn't, you need to take a break and do something else."

Stanley Cup–winning coach MARC CRAWFORD on confidence:

"When you're playing to win you don't change your game, you go out and make things happen, like making a good pass. If you're playing not to lose, you don't take many chances and you don't challenge the defensive team much—basically, you get into the neutral zone and dump it into the offensive zone. There's not much thought when you're playing not to lose. Confidence is a funny thing. You can't just give it to somebody; they have to earn it."

playing big

▲ RYAN SMYTH

Hockey is not for everybody. You have to love to compete, and you have to enjoy the contact. At every level and every position, hockey is a test of courage.

Every surface on a hockey rink is hard. The game is played on ice. The rink is framed by boards made of rigid wood timbers, covered with thick plastic and topped with hardened glass. The goal is made of welded steel. The object of the game is to move a hardened rubber puck that can cause damage even when it hits you on the pads. Players wear razor-sharp skates and use sticks made of wood and metal to control the puck. Equipment is so solid that it can hurt opponents. Any of these objects and materials can injure you. No other game is played in such rugged conditions.

Add body contact at combined speeds of 30 mph, and have 10 skaters chase a three-inch-diameter disc that flies around faster than the highway speed limit—it's a recipe for excitement.

There are risks in playing hockey. Risks can be lessened, though. The way to make hockey safe and fun is to play the game right.

Careless or harmful use of sticks causes more injuries than body contact does. You are responsible for the harm your stick causes, even if it is by accident. Don't carry your stick high. Use it for what it's intended for. Keep your stickblade close to the ice. When your stick becomes caught in an opponent's equipment or mask, drop it. Just let it go.

Full-contact hockey starts for most players around 12 years of age. Contact adds another skill to the game: the ability to take and give a clean body check. If you want to make contact, you have to take contact. Never hit an opponent from behind. Never leave your feet to make a hit. Keep your elbows to yourself. Let the referee call the game.

"Playing tough doesn't mean fighting," says Martin Lapointe. "When you play tough, you go in the corners and dig the puck out, and you get your nose dirty."

The body contact in hockey is part of the fun. Even when body checking is not allowed, players run into each other. It just happens.

In the National Hockey League, most players welcome contact. We say they "play big." At any level, playing big means enjoying the contact and playing the game right.

KEITH TKACHUK goes to the net:

"First, the way I look at it is that if you want to score goals and play hard, you have to go to the net. That is where all of the goals come from. You just have to stick it out and play as hard as you can. If you do that everything else will take care of itself."

How SHAYNE CORSON made the 1998 Olympics:

"One of the keys is to concentrate on playing two-way hockey. I've always tried to do that. I take pride in my defensive game and always work on my defensive skills. Being able to play more than one position (centre or wing) is also very beneficial."

How goalie OLAF KOLZIG plays big for big minutes: ➤

"I'm able to play as many minutes as I do because I take care of myself. I train hard in the summer and throughout the season, and I watch what I eat. The key is to have strong legs and a strong core, and to limit the groin and stomach injuries that a goalie usually faces. My advice to young goalies is not to overtrain. Your bodies are still growing and adjusting."

DAVE MANSON says: ➤

"You have to have respect for an opponent. The minute you show disrespect towards an opponent is when somebody gets hurt."

RYAN SMYTH is immovable:

"Create a foundation for yourself so that the opposition has a hard time moving you. I like to use my stick and legs to maintain my balance, giving me the stability to stand strong in front of the net. Mobility, flexibility and body control are also key, as you need to be able to react quickly and know how to manoeuvre your body so that you can be first to the puck."

◄ PETER FORSBERG is a rare top-scorer who plays big:

"Look at the holes and not at the goalie. Think shoot first. If you see an opening, that's when you can deke, like when the goalie's too far out."

ERIC DAZE on playing big but penalty-free:

"To play physically and stay out of the penalty box, you have to practise finishing your check while you're skating."

Defensive defenseman BOB BOUGHNER on body checking:

"I have to be physical every night. It's not about fighting or whipping your gloves off every night. It's about playing a physical style, especially in your own end."

JAROME IGINLA gets physical:

"Penalties such as tripping or hooking can be avoided by skating harder to catch your check, or by being in the proper position, so that you don't have to pull your check down."

47

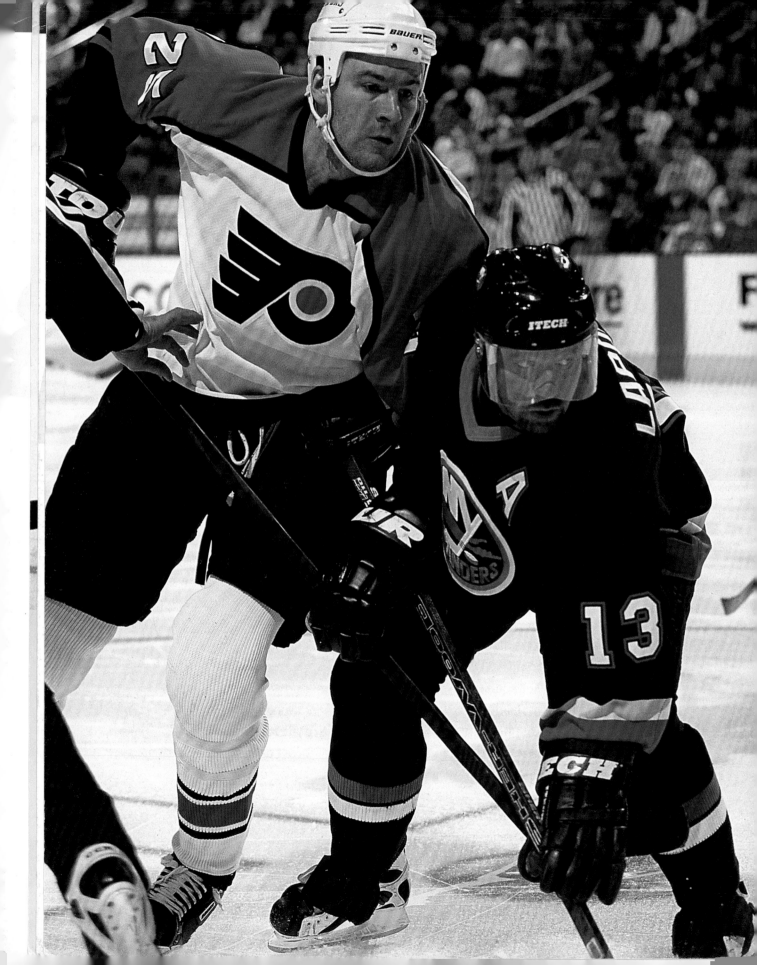

Centre STEVE REINPRECHT
lets the puck do the work:

"Let the puck do the work for you. Making a
few passes will get your opponents on their
heels. Try to get the puck to the player where
he can handle it. It doesn't always have to
be on the tape."

PHIL HOUSLEY on the breakout pass:

"For a defenseman, it's very important to get to the puck as quickly as
possible to give you more time to evaluate your options. This goes for
both your own end and the neutral zone. Before you get to the puck,
know what you want to do with it. Have options in mind. Remember to
keep your head up to look for your teammates, and make all your
passes hard to avoid having them picked off."

◄ **KEITH PRIMEAU on being versatile:**

"I am a natural centre. I played a little left wing when
I was in Detroit. That's what makes championship teams,
when everyone can adjust to different positions."

DARIUS KASPARAITIS on listening to his goalie:

"I love playing with Garth Snow because he always
communicates with us, and it's easier for defensemen to
play when the goalie talks. Sometimes he plays the puck,
too. That makes our life easier."

How to win faceoffs, by TRAVIS GREEN:

"On faceoffs you might try your backhand with a player,
and if that isn't working, you might have to change it up
and go with your forehand. Practise different drills with
your buddies. It's also important to talk to other players
to see what's working and what isn't."

STEVE RUCCHIN on not losing twice on defensive zone faceoffs:

"You're never going to win every faceoff, but if there's one place you don't want to lose one, it's in your own zone. If you lose the faceoff, your job isn't over. You have to make sure the other centreman doesn't go to the net unopposed. Use your body position to contain him and to keep him to the outside. You need to work; it won't come easily but as long as your effort is greater than his, you'll get the job done."

DENNIS BONVIE on making the best of things:

"Obviously, I want to play every game and I want to go out and play a regular shift, but that's not the case. If they ask me to go out and play one shift, I'm going to play it as hard as I can. I'm going to do it to the best of my ability. That's all I can do. I want to be here, and I want to add what I can add to the team."

Goalie RON TUGNUTT talks to the D: ➤

"Many times the goaltender has to be the defensemen's eyes. One way is by telling them what to do so that they can make the right play to get the puck out of the zone. Off the ice, I tell them about how I'd like them to react to certain situations, like rebounds, men in front of the net and breakaways. That way we're on the same page."

Dr. CURTIS JOSEPH, goalie and PhD from Doghouse U:

"There's nothing worse than being doubted by your coach or by your teammates. You have to keep your chin up, keep playing and improve yourself in practice. Try to take some positives out of it, because it will make you a better person and a better player. It will also help you mentally to develop a thick skin."

ERIC LACROIX, on playing for his father, GM Pierre Lacroix:

"You've got to have the confidence of your teammates that you're pulling your weight. They need to know that you will go to battle for them every night. Regardless of who the coach is, show up to practice and to play hard and fair."

What coach KEN HITCHCOCK looks for in a leader:

"A leader's first and foremost obligation to the team is to perform at a high level, no matter what his playing ability may be. A leader must also have the pulse of the team, which is being tuned in to bringing important information to the players and the coaches."

MARK MESSIER on leadership:

"To be a good leader, you have to earn the respect of your teammates, which can only be done by working hard on the ice and carrying yourself in a positive manner off the ice. The players have to know that you will sacrifice anything for the good of the team, and that you will stand up for them in any situation."

◄ Captain MATS SUNDIN sets the tone:

"One thing a captain can do to make his team better is to lead by example, both on and off the ice. It's also very important to establish a dressing room where every player puts the team first."

VALERI BURE on his first 35-goal season:

"My success is a result of confidence in myself and of people believing in me. My linemates play an extremely important role. They're very important as they support me at all times on the ice. Confidence and success go hand in hand, but it's difficult to have one without the other."

special thanks

Many people helped with the sizeable research effort that resulted in this book. Thanks, first and foremost, to all the National Hockey League players who shared their experiences and playing tips.

For his unfailing enthusiasm, his meticulous research and his dedication to this project since Day One, a heartfelt thank you to Mike Harling. Special thanks also to Denise Gomez and Jamey Horan of the NHL and to Todd Sharrock of the Columbus Blue Jackets.

Rob Viccars, T.C. Carling and Chris Brumwell of the Vancouver Canucks were unfailingly helpful. Brad Pascall and André Brin of Hockey Canada and Heather Ahearn of USA Hockey arranged access to non-NHL players. Tim Wharnsby of the NHL Players Association and Jim Nice of the RBRT Sports Group helped find players who changed clubs during this project.

On behalf of the clubs: Ken Arnold, San Jose Sharks; Tom Enders and Eric McGraw, Phoenix Coyotes; Heidi Holland, Boston Bruins; Tony Ommen, Chicago Blackhawks; Zack Hill, Philadelphia Flyers; Jay Preble, Tampa Bay Lightning; Jason Vogel, New York Rangers; Mark Janko, Dallas Stars; Kevin Wiles, Buffalo Sabres; Merit Tully, Anaheim Mighty Ducks; Brian Potter, Washington Capitals; Phil Legault, Ottawa Senators; Kyle S. Hanlin, Carolina Hurricanes; Beau Topar, L.A. Kings; Steve Bovino, Pittsburgh Penguins; Kevin Dessart, New Jersey Devils; Dominick Saillant, Club de hockey Canadien; Dave Griffiths, Toronto Maple Leafs; Warren Suitor, Edmonton Oilers; Frank Buonomo, Nashville Predators; Rocky Bonanno, New York Islanders; Peter Hanlon, Calgary Flames; Stanley Richardson, St. Louis Blues; Michael Citro, Florida Panthers; and Matthew Davis, Kansas City Blades Hockey Club.

Thanks again, as always, to our friends at Cyclone Taylor Sports, Vancouver, who have supported the *Hockey the NHL Way* series from the beginning.